# The World is Binary:

*Why Love is the Answer*

So much of life is defined by binary concepts. Religion speaks of good and evil. Science explores truth and falsehood. Computers are denoted by 1's and 0's. We can see it everywhere, and it affects everything. This book explores the idea that these divisions may not be as clear as they appear to be, and also some ideas on how we can bridge the gap. It is presented that there are two emotions influencing human behavior, love and fear, which gives rise to our greatest pleasure and pain, both on an individual level and as a society. While both must exist in some equilibrium, the book suggests that choosing love over fear can lead to a happier, more fulfilling life, and also a better world.

I introduce here the idea that there are two fundamental forces in the world, love and fear. These are distinct from the physical and chemical manifestation of emotion, what we feel when we love someone or fear something. My argument is that these forces exist as abstract concepts, independent of human emotion, similar to how a mathematical concept can exist and be true even without a thinker. It is not necessary to prescribe to any particular spiritual or scientific sect. In this case, these concepts apply universally. However, an open mind is required since it is not possible, at least with current technology, to prove these theories empirically.

The basic premise is that there are essentially only two forces of nature, which I am calling love and fear. These forces influence all conscious beings, to some extent, and are the source of our greatest pleasure and pain, both on an individual level and as a society. Both forces must exist and some sense of balance must be maintained. Without one or the other, then nothing would exist. Similar to how lightness can only be experienced if there is a concept of darkness. The contrast between light and dark is what allows either to exist at all. One force can become more dominant, for a certain period of time, but an equilibrium will always be met, sooner or later.

While I am calling these elements love and fear, these are merely the symbols that I've adopted, that are comfortable for my mode of thinking. If you are a spiritual person, you can alternatively think of them as good and evil. For a philosopher, maybe moral and immoral would make more sense. As a scientist, true and false. To a computer (if some AI is reading this in the future), 1 and 0. Or on a more practical level, they could be pleasure and pain. It really doesn't make much difference, they are simply symbols pointing to the same thing. However, labeling something good or evil is a moral distinction. In my argument, the elements themselves are neither moral nor immoral, they just exist, but their manifestation can have moral consequence.

To illustrate this point, think of a common saying that money is evil. Well currency is simply a way to trade, or represent value. It would be akin to saying a mathematical formula was evil, which would clearly be nonsense. The next step would be to say the love of money is evil. This doesn't make sense either. If we establish that money itself is not evil, how could loving a neutral concept then be evil? What I suggest is that the issue is an imbalance. The love of money, but without a corresponding love for humanity or for the environment, is what makes it evil. For example, con artists that swindle victims out of their life savings, or people polluting the environment for financial gain. In this situation, the motivator is still love, in essence, but one that is out of balance, due to the lack of love for their fellow humans or the Earth.

The same can also be true of fear. If you are walking down the street and actively look both ways to ensure you are not hit by a car, this can be a healthy fear. And the root of that fear may not itself be negative. In fact, it may be motivated by love. For example, the love of life, or the love for your family. Though the emotion of fear is real, in this instance, the fear that if you were to be injured or killed you could not provide for your family. But if you get to the root of the matter, it is actually the love of your family that generated the conditions for fear to exist. So in this way, same as the unscrupulous business person, we are all motivated by love and it's not a clear case that love is always good and fear is always bad. The important part is that there is a healthy equilibrium.

I will clarify that while I believe these elements exist on their own, the precise mechanism of their manifestation is likely psychological. One way to consider it is that within our mind are two balancing forces, of love and fear, and you could even think of them as two independent conscious minds. Meaning they may have their own thoughts, desires, and will. What we experience is merely the equilibrium of these forces, so this is not so different than traditional theories of psychoanalysis.

One other way to consider this phenomenon is to think in terms of freedom and control. One side is moving toward freedom and expression, with the other toward control and order. The freedom can express many things. This can be an intellectual freedom, to consider radical modes of thinking that lead to scientific breakthrough. An artistic expression that leads to creating works of art or original ideas that move people. A sexual type of freedom in terms of acceptance of yourself, in addition to others that are unlike you. Or it could be more on a practical level, the freedom to choose what you do with your time and your life.

In terms of control, this is used to balance out the freedom. A system with complete freedom, as in no rules, would not be stable. For example, some amount of radical thinking is necessary to make scientific breakthroughs, in the cases of things like quantum mechanics. However if the thinking is so radical that it contradicts everything before it (and the scientific method) then it is likely not to lead to stable results (even if the line of thinking is correct). To put another way, imagine you are in an argument with a close friend. You may think in your mind of something really hurtful you could say to them. If you were acting purely out of freedom, you might say that hurtful thing. But the other side of control would balance out and lead to an understanding that you may hurt the other person disproportionate to what they said to you, or that it would damage the relationship, or have other undesirable consequences. Which would stop you from saying those things.

I'd like to be clear that this is not just a book about theory. This is a book about action and the change you can take in your life. While I am positing that the emotions do not have a moral basis, I do believe that to lead a happy and fulfilling life, you want to strive toward love. Love for yourself, and for your fellow humans, and also animals and plant life. It is not necessary to meditate for years, or dedicate your life to a religious sect. In fact, I would say you don't have to be religious at all, though these actions are fully compatible with popular religions and will even work if you don't believe in any particular faith.

To illustrate this further, aim to give love and gratitude to everyone you interact with. This obviously means your family and friends, but also your coworkers, strangers on the street or on the internet, basically anywhere you go. For example, when I go grocery shopping, I say hello and smile to the people stocking the shelves, because I appreciate that without their hard work I would not have food to eat. I spark conversations with the cashiers and treat them with respect and as equals. Even a short conversation and a compliment can brighten their day. I generously give to the homeless on the street, because they are people equal to anyone else and deserve respect. Just as an anecdote, I once gave a homeless man $40 on Christmas Eve. It was cold and he was begging on the street. So I decided to hand him two $20 bills and say Merry Christmas. And his eyes lit up, he was so happy for a moment and astonished at the act of generosity. And I was happy too, as he smiled and said something really nice to me. And in that moment, we both felt some love, and probably for the remainder of the night as well. To be honest, it's entirely possible that the man bought illicit substances with the money, but that is not any of my concern. The point was to increase love and happiness in the world, and I'm sure that was accomplished, at least for that brief moment on Christmas Eve.

You don't even need to interact with other people to practice this, you can do it with yourself. For example, let's say you are eating dinner. You can be grateful that food exists (whether you believe in God or nature), you can be grateful that the farmers were able to harvest the crops, that there are drivers that transported the food from faraway places, that the government created the roads and highway systems to transport the goods, that you yourself have the money to buy the food, and a safe space to eat it, and so on. If you do this, the food will actually taste better. In fact, very often I am certain I am eating the best meal of my life, and then tomorrow again I will be eating the best meal of my life. It certainly feels that way. The key is that it's not a logical process, you cannot just think it, or even have faith in it, it won't work. You have to feel it. The thinking mind is not part of the process at all. It is difficult to pinpoint precisely how this change happens. At first you may simply be thinking something because you read it in a book, but you don't actually believe it. Next, you can start believing in it, or even have faith that it works, but this is still not enough. The key is simply feeling it, which is not something I can explain. But if you can eliminate fear in your life, or at least reduce it so it is not overpowering, then you should be ready to experience it. For example, the fear that these techniques won't work for you, the fear that you don't deserve it, and so on. These are the things that are holding you back.

And this applies to everything, even on the internet. I always spread love and thank people or praise them for their art or their contributions. Even small comments telling people you like what they did, or that they are amazing, or whatever, can brighten their day. And I generally only give 5 star reviews. Even if something had some small faults, I will look at the things about the product or service that made me happy and focus on that. Clearly, sometimes there are products that are broken, or don't work for whatever reason, so I won't leave a review. That said, there have been some rare cases where I've given lower scores, but I will write specifically the pros and cons of the product and give a fair assessment. I think of the big picture. By giving a glowing review, you are spreading love. The seller or manufacturer will become happier, their sales may increase, other buyers may have renewed confidence in a product they wanted to buy, and so on. However, leaving a 1 star review out of spite is spreading fear. For example, the seller may fear that people will then not buy the product (leading to fear that they will go out of business). Potential buyers may have wanted the product (and it may have suited their specific needs well) but reading a bad review will give them fear the product is not good (or fear they won't be able to find what they are looking for), and so on. And this really accomplishes nothing besides making everyone involved, including yourself, more unhappy. So it is not productive.

These concepts can also be applied to bigger goals. As an example, I don't believe that protesting or political arguments, for example, engaging in a fight with someone with differing ideological opinions, accomplishes anything. In fact, I think it increases the amount of fear and unhappiness in the world. What I am saying is that posting hateful things on social media does not actually change anything. It amplifies the fear that already exists, for example, the fear of the other, fear that things are out of control, fear of societal collapse, and so on. Instead of fighting, you should aim to love others that disagree with your beliefs. Try to listen to them and understand them, and find common ground that you can agree upon (meaning things you both love). We are all human, and, on a basic level, all want the same things. So there is no need to fight at all, we are in this together as a team. Instead of thinking of it as a battle, consider it a play. The point isn't to win (because there will never be a conclusive winner or loser) but to simply make it look good, and enjoy life in the process. While we can disagree, and never ultimately come to a truce, there is no need to attack each other. All we do is hurt ourselves, the other person, and the system as a whole. Instead, we can support the causes we believe in (which will never be universally agreed upon) but in a positive way out of love. As a way to help people, not hurt them. This is paramount and the essence of the message here.

I would like to expand on the point about protesting. There have certainly been protests that worked. We can look back at the civil rights movement, woman's rights, and, more recently, the LGBTQ movement. However, I don't believe that signing a petition, or going outside with a poster and screaming, actually changes anything. In reality, it may make the situation worse (particularly with the recent trend of illegal protesting or riots). What this does is create further division, through the increase of fear. The fear that your side will lose, the fear that the world is out of control, and so on. What I believe is that real change does not happen with logical arguments. Making a case for your position, even if it is logically sound, will not change someone's mind. However, movements that invoke a feeling of love can, as they speak to emotion.

We can bring this back to a more relevant experience, personal success. I've had a long and rather successful career, and I attribute this mostly to me making bold and risky moves. I've cycled through many different jobs and roles in different industries, I've moved to different cities, I've been open to new opportunities. At some times I have been working for a stable company and a new offer will come in, like for a fresh start-up. For me this is exciting, because I look at the opportunity and chance of something positive happening. And this comes from love. However, I would discuss the choice with a friend or family member, and they may focus on the fear and attempt to talk me out of it. The fear that the company could lose funding or go out of business, the fear that I could not make new friends in a new city. And while it is good to consider all possibilities, it is important not to give the doom prognostications too much weight. For example, instead of imagining all the bad things that could happen (which may even be highly unlikely or unrealistic), why not think of the positives? What if the new company is a huge success? What if I meet new people that are even more in line with my thinking and values than my old friends? What if I become more happy in the process? This is important to consider. Additionally, even if those unlikely doom scenarios do come to pass, they are usually not even that bad. I've worked at start-ups that went bust. I've been fired from my job. And it wasn't a big deal. Usually some other opportunity would appear at just the right moment, and everything was fine, sometimes even much better than before. Because there was no fear. I trusted that things were okay and as they should be. Oftentimes it is the fear itself that can influence your behavior, making the doom scenarios more likely to happen. If you are acting out of love, then it is more likely that the positive benefit will materialize.

Another point I would like to make, is that I believe the other feelings we experience are rooted in the core of love and fear. As an example, surprise can be a love of the unexpected, while anxiety can be a fear of the unknown. In this way, I suggest that hate does not actually exist and is only fear. You may believe to hate some other, as in hating a different ethnic group or people of a certain sexual orientation. But this is really fear. In the case of ethnicity, you may fear that another race will take your job, or that a prevalence of another group will dilute your culture or heritage, and so on. With sexual orientation, it's possible you adhere to strict concepts of sex or gender and fear that developments in this area will destroy your own values. Or it could be a personal fear. If the boundaries, let's say, between a man and a woman were to be blurred, how could you be sure who you were attracted to? In which case it would be a fear of losing your own sexual orientation. This can be applied really to any binary division, such as supporting a particular political party or the debate between people of faith and the scientific community. In a way, it is not necessarily hating another, it is a fear of losing your own identity, which comes back again to love. The idea of preserving the values and things that you love and you stand for.

One particular phenomenon that I find troubling is the use of hate speech on the internet. It is very common, at least in my experience, particularly in communities that are essentially unmoderated, like online video games. You could join a game server and, within minutes, hear the most offensive racial slurs, sexist comments, as well as homophobic or transphobic sentiments. This is what results from a completely free system, a system where anyone can say whatever they want, with apparent impunity, however hurtful they may be. As I have stated before, I don't believe hate exists, this is a promotion of fear. In the case of these hateful comments, the victim may fear they are unwelcome on the internet, or in society at large, fear that people will not accept them, fear that the system is broken. Complete freedom is not advantageous to the balance, and, in many other areas, not desirable either, particularly if it violates other freedoms. Case in point, you are not free to punch someone on the street for no reason, you are not free to steal someone's car, even if you so desire. This is not a freedom of speech issue, as there are clear limits in place for dangerous actions. But it seems that the society values physical freedoms over mental and psychological ones. If you were to be assaulted on the street, you would have a clear case. However if someone harasses you, racially, sexually, or otherwise, this seems to be no issue at all. And I think this needs to change. First in people recognizing the severity of the psychological damage caused, and also in both the private and public sector taking definitive action.

To give you a little backstory, today I would consider myself a deeply spiritual person. But I don't subscribe to any specific religion, though I have explored many (both Eastern and Western). As a child I attended a private religious school, but I don't recall ever having faith. And as a young adult, I renounced religion, and studied science for many years. As I got older, I felt something was missing in my life, and also had some extraordinary experiences that made me wonder if there was something more. So I got interested in Eastern religion and also philosophy (both modern and ancient) and explored a variety of topics. From everything I read I think I did gain insight, though I did not take any one book as truth. I believe they are all true, in that they point to something greater or at least provide you with guidance in your life. During that same time, I have studied many forms of science and mathematics, from ancient text all the way up to the cutting edge of quantum mechanics. And I believe all of that to be true as well. The important part is that this knowledge helps us navigate the world. For example, science can teach us how to build a computer, or allow us to communicate with people all over the world instantly. And religion and philosophy can teach us how to be kinder to each other, or to discover insights about ourselves and the world that are not easily measured with technology. It is important to find this equilibrium that is beneficial to the system. And the system can refer to many things. It can be you as an individual, your community, your country, or the world itself.

One thing I've come to understand as I've become older is the importance of order. This is another binary: freedom and order. As we see now with modern technology, ideas are spreading faster than ever. Something can happen on the other side of the world and, by the next day, everyone knows about it. This is both amazing and gravely dangerous. While I absolutely support free information, I also respect order. In this day and age, it has become increasingly difficult to determine what is true or false, or if two opposing ideas are both true or both false. Computer graphics can create images and videos that are indistinguishable from real life. Anyone with access to the internet and some basic design skills can prop up a website in a few hours that looks legitimate. And viral social media posts can spread widely in hours, with no basis in reality. It actually doesn't matter which political ideology you believe in, it is difficult for anyone to tell what is truth. While there are definitely sources of news that you can verify are more trustworthy than others, it still doesn't stop the spread of information, or the social division between people with opposing beliefs. Traditionally this was the role of the government and the media, to make sure people were getting relevant news stories and also guiding the discussion in ways that were beneficial to the society. While some people may believe this is biased, for example, you can find stories on an international news outlet that didn't make it to the domestic news, this is actually a very important concept to maintain order. Even in recent times, before the explosion of the internet, there was simply too much information. Not every single event could be reported on, and some stories could be disruptive to the order. And the order is of great importance. This is the stability in the system. In the social contract, the rule of law, in economic systems, and so on. So this equilibrium must also be maintained. However not at the total expense of freedom, as there must be a balance. What I suggest is that people, especially the ones with radical ideas, understand that unconstrained freedom would not be stable, or beneficial to anyone on any side. I don't believe this is a case of right and wrong. What I believe is that stability of the system helps everyone and going too far in either direction, meaning anarchy or totalitarianism, will break the fabric of society. But I also don't believe there can be any winners or losers, and the system will eventually ebb and flow and balance out, but only over time. There can still be significant periods of imbalance. This is key to understand.

To get back to some of the more abstract concepts, and why I think love and fear exist without necessarily a physical emotion, we can look at other systems. For this point, we can explore the idea of a free market and the invisible hand. Basically, in a free market, the balance between supply and demand should create a natural equilibrium that is beneficial to the society. But where exactly is this invisible hand? Is it in the minds of the people, or does it exist elsewhere, possibly in the complex interactions of the whole? In theory, it's great, and has been proven to work. However, a completely free market would be out of balance. In practice, there must be rules. For example, there could be laws that maintain a minimum wage, that limit the amount of overtime (or, at least, require compensation), that some actions are off-limits, like child labor, or that certain agreements are considered illegal, such as we see with anti-competitive laws. As I have stated, the key is in balance and equilibrium. While there can be some debate about specific rules, such as the rate of the minimum wage, it should be evident that the concept of a minimum wage at all is beneficial. So, in this way, the order does, in fact, remove freedom from the system, but in a manner that actually helps society.

Let's look now at some simple things you can do to implement these concepts, the idea of love, into your life. First, you can call your parents (if they are still with us) and tell them you love them. If you have children, let them know how much you appreciate them. Text a friend you haven't spoken to recently and catch up. If you live with animals, pet them. Give them some treats and tell them you love them. These things don't cost any money, and might only take a few minutes of your time, but they can brighten someone's day. Say hello to someone in your community you might not have met before, and be kind. Open up to people, even strangers. This is another form of fear. The fear of rejection, fear that you might say the wrong thing or offend someone. But if you speak honestly, and out of love, most people will be accepting as they can see you are in earnest. You don't have to tell everyone your whole life's story, but don't hold back either. Speak your mind. You'd be surprised what people know or what they are willing to tell you back. This doesn't have to be exclusively in the physical world. When you are online, try to be kind to everyone you interact with. Look carefully at the words you type. Your choice of words can make all the difference. Try to avoid using negative words, and if you can't find the right word, choose another topic you can speak about positively. Find something to love, and focus on that. The words themselves are symbols, but they hold power in their association. So aiming to use only positive words can make a big difference. And if you do this for a day, you can affect all the people important in your life. If you do this everyday, then everyone around you will be happier, happier to have you in their life, and you will be happier yourself. And maybe they will pick up on it and try it too. If everyone did this, everyday, then the whole world would change overnight.

Another thing you can practice is gratitude. You can do this if you are in a romantic relationship, by realizing your partner is the most amazing person in the world. If you have children, they are the greatest children in the world. If you have pets, they are the best pets in the world. This, on the surface, does not appear to make sense, but it does. You see, I'm a cat person. And I truly believe that my cat is the best cat in the world. Objectively, this clearly can't be true. As in, she is not the fastest cat in the world, or maybe her fur is not the most intricate pattern, and so on. However, I love her more than any cat I know, and I can't imagine loving another cat more, so, at least to me, she's the best. The same can be true for your lover or for your family. It's not a logical argument or some sort of comparison. It is about fully embracing love unconditionally. If you can do these things, you will see your life change. You will become happier and more content. For others around you, their lives too will be improved, and there can be real changes in a relationship, as long as it is based on love.

In summary, the world around us is defined by binary concepts. However, it is not clear that one side is inherently better than another. These elements exist in an equilibrium, and both must exist, there can be no winners or losers. This applies to everything, from the ideological differences of science and religion, the people's freedom and the government's order, as well as to the emotional balance of individuals and the system as a whole. What I suggest is that there is no right or wrong, no need to fight, and no logical argument that will ever sway either side. The importance is in the balance, which we can only maintain by realizing we are working together and are all one and part of a single system of this Earth. And while we can disagree, and accept we will never agree, we should put aside our differences and work together for a better future.